W9-BXL-572

WHAT IF I'M WORRIED ABOUT
COVID-19?

Bookmobile
Fountaindale Public Library
Bolingbrook, IL
(630) 759-2102

By Emily Dolbear

The Child's World®
childsworld.com

Published by The Child's World®
1980 Lookout Drive
Mankato, MN 56003-1705
800-599-READ
www.childsworld.com

Photos ©: Daisy Daisy/Shutterstock.
com: 6; digitalskillet/Shutterstock.
com: 15;FamVeld/Shutterstock.com:
8; fizkes/Shutterstock.com: cover, 2,
13, 22; Maria Symchych/
Shutterstock.com: 11; Monkey
Business Images/Shutterstock.com:
5; Oleksii Synelnykov/
Shutterstock.com: 19; pixfly/
Shutterstock.com: 16

ISBN 9781503853188
(Reinforced Library Binding)

ISBN 9781503853201
(Portable Document Format)

ISBN 9781503853263
(Online Multi-user eBook)

LCCN: 2020939104

Printed in the United
States of America

About the Author
Emily J. Dolbear writes
and edits books from
her home in Brookline,
Massachusetts. She
lives with her family
and their dog, who has
provided much comfort
during COVID-19.

CONTENTS

CHAPTER ONE

Be Informed

If you are worried about the disease called COVID-19, you are not alone. You might feel sad or frustrated. You might feel angry sometimes. Getting information about what's happening can help calm you down.

In 2020, millions of people around the world became sick with this disease. There is no cure. Scientists are working on a COVID-19 **vaccine**. Vaccines protect people from deadly diseases.

Scientists continue to learn about COVID-19. But they know some important facts. COVID-19 is caused by a coronavirus first discovered in 2019. A coronavirus is a type of **virus** that affects birds and **mammals**. COVID-19 spreads easily from person to person.

COVID-19 has caused both adults and children to worry about lots of things.

Washing your hands with soap for 20 seconds kills the coronavirus that causes COVID-19.

People with COVID-19 often have a fever and a dry cough. They feel very tired. They may have body pain or a sore throat. In some cases, it becomes difficult to breathe. Others with COVID-19 have mild symptoms or none at all.

The best virus prevention is regular handwashing. If you have no soap and water, use hand sanitizer containing at least 60 percent alcohol. Try not to touch your mouth, nose, or eyes. That keeps germs from spreading.

Stay home as much as you can. That prevents the spread of COVID-19 in your community. When you do go outside, wearing a face mask can help protect yourself and others. Put at least 6 feet (2 meters) between you and other people.

COVID-19 FACT

The name COVID-19 comes from the letters in the words "**co**rona **vi**rus **d**isease 20**19**." The year 2019 is when the virus was discovered.

Sharing your feelings with family members can make you feel better when you are stuck at home.

CHAPTER TWO

Understand and Share Your Feelings

COVID-19 altered life in a short time. Schools shut down to protect you and others. Large gatherings were canceled. Special events you were looking forward to were called off. Malls closed and playgrounds emptied. You lost the chance to play and watch team sports.

Your family may have limited their trips to the grocery store. Playing with friends the way you used to wasn't possible. Staying home prevents the spread of the virus.

COVID-19 forced everyone to change their behavior. They learned new things quickly. Everyone washes their hands. Face masks are common. People are careful not to stand close to each other when they go out.

Businesses have had to change how they operate. Many grown-ups work from home. Students like you connected with your teachers and classmates online. You changed how you communicated with family and friends outside your home. Video calls, texting, and email became the safest way to be in touch.

COVID-19 FACT

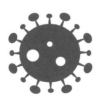

Every U.S. state closed their school buildings. More than 55 million students were affected. That doesn't include students at colleges and universities.

Learning from home was hard for many students at first.

The sudden changes during a crisis like COVID-19 can cause **anxiety**. It's natural to worry about the unknown. It takes time to adjust to new things.

Sometimes it's hard to talk about your feelings. But sharing your worries can make you feel better. Other times, just being with someone who cares about you can cheer you up.

The time of COVID-19 is no different. You might play a game or listen to music with a family member. Go for a walk or bike ride with a parent. Or you might enjoy doing a special project together. You are not alone in your worry.

COVID-19 FACT

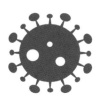

Can you get COVID-19 from your pet? Probably not. Treat your pet as you do your family group. Don't let your pet play with people or animals outside of your family group.

Tell adults about your feelings. They can help you to understand your emotions.

CHAPTER THREE

Take Care of Yourself

Everyone needs a daily plan and things to do. It's important to sleep and eat well. Fresh air and exercise are always good for you.

Remember to keep up with your schoolwork. Try writing down some thoughts in a journal. Find an interesting book or magazine to read. Watch movies too. Practice a musical instrument or learn to dribble a ball. Draw or paint something. Look for a fun puzzle. Rest when you are tired. Be sure to ask for support when you need it.

Getting the right amount of sleep helps relax your body and mind. It helps your body stay healthy, too.

Doing yoga outside is a great way to relax your body and stay calm.

When you worry, you might feel it in your body. It might be hard to sleep or concentrate. You might have a headache or pain in your stomach.

Deep breathing is one way to calm your body. Try breathing in slowly through your nose. Then breathe out slowly through your mouth. Do this three times. How do you feel?

Learn to stretch and strengthen your body. That's another way to improve how you feel. Try some **yoga** exercises with a family member. Yoga uses meditation. That is when you focus your mind on calming thoughts. Yoga helps people become fit and relaxed.

COVID-19 FACT

Yoga began long ago in India. It uses deep breathing and slow stretching or exercise movements.

CHAPTER FOUR

What Else Can I Do?

Coping with uncertainty is a challenge. Do you know someone who is worried about COVID-19? You could make a cheerful card for a nurse or doctor who lives nearby. You could be in touch with a relative you haven't talked to lately.

When you support other people, you feel better too. Being kind to others is always a good choice. And staying involved keeps you from worrying.

Making cards for doctors and nurses is a great way to stay busy and not worry so much.

Why not enjoy the slower pace of life at home? You could offer to do an activity with a brother or sister. Take care of the family pets. Put away your things without being asked. You might want to help make dinner or a dessert.

Certain things may still seem overwhelming. Some anxiety is a normal part of living. It's true that everyone worries. Giving and asking for support from the people around us helps get through difficult times.

COVID-19 FACT

People around the world celebrate International Nurses Day on May 12. May 12, 2020 was the 200th anniversary of Florence Nightingale's birth. She was the founder of modern nursing.

THINK ABOUT IT

There are lots of things you can do at home while keeping yourself and others safe.

1. Start a journal. Think of three things that you are grateful for each day. Could you list or draw them?

2. Do some online research about yoga for beginners. Ask an adult to help you. Learn three poses and teach them to the people in your home.

3. Imagine an entire Saturday with no electronic devices. Plan a schedule of fun screen-free activities for your family.

GOOD NEWS!

Most people had to visit an office to see a doctor before COVID-19. Healthcare workers now meet with their patients over the Internet. This helps to reduce the spread of the virus. Patients can discuss symptoms and get prescriptions without leaving their homes. Using a computer or smartphone for routine medical care is called **telemedicine**.

There will always be visits to the doctor's office and the hospital. But many patients like how easy the online option is. Telemedicine visits could reach 1 billion in 2020. This is some good news during COVID-19.

GLOSSARY

anxiety (ang-ZY-uh-tee) Anxiety is a feeling of fear or worry. Both children and adults experience anxiety.

mammals (MAM-ullz) Mammals are animals that have warm bodies and feed their babies milk from their bodies. People are mammals.

telemedicine (TEL-uh-MED-ih-sin) Using a computer, a tablet, or a smartphone to provide routine medical care is called telemedicine.

vaccine (vak-SEEN) A vaccine is a weakened or dead form of a disease that is swallowed or injected into a person. This causes their body to fight the germs, and gives them the ability to fight that disease's germs if the body comes in contact with them again.

virus (VY-russ) A virus is a very tiny organism that causes diseases. A virus can only be seen with a special kind of microscope.

yoga (YOH-guh) Yoga is a type of training for the body and the mind. Yoga uses stretching and meditation— focusing your mind on calming thoughts. Yoga helps people become relaxed and fit.

TO LEARN MORE

IN THE LIBRARY

Latta, Sara. *What is COVID-19?*
Mankato, MN: The Child's World, 2021.

Percival, Tom. *Ruby Finds a Worry.*
New York, NY: Bloomsbury, 2019.

Wallace, Adam M. *The Day My Kids Stayed
Home: Explaining COVID-19 and the Corona
Virus to Your Kids*. Adam M. Wallace, 2020.

ON THE WEB

Visit our Web site for links about COVID-19:

childsworld.com/links

Note to Parents, Teachers, and Librarians: We routinely verify our Web links to make sure they are safe and active sites. So encourage your readers to check them out!

INDEX